The Pendle Witches

•

RICHARD CATLOW

Published by Hendon Publishing Co. Ltd., Hendon Mill, Nelson, Lancashire.

© Richard Catlow, 1976.
First Edition, April, 1976.
Second impression, April, 1983.
Third impression, April, 1986.
Fourth impression, April, 1991.
Fifth impression, March, 1994.
Sixth impression, February, 1998.
Seventh impression, June, 1999.

Printed by Turner & Earnshaw Limited, Westway House, Sycamore Avenue, Burnley, Lancashire.

Introduction

"Ingleborough, Pendle and Penyghent,
Are the highest hills between Scotland and Trent."

The words are those of an old North Country proverb which like many proverbs, if not strictly true, contains some grain of truth. None of the hills comes near to being the biggest in the North and at 1830 feet Pendle is lower than many Pennine and Lakeland hills.

But in one way the rhyme is right, for each of the hills is something special. Pendle is especially worthy of note. Cut off from the Pennine Chain—a sort of missing link—it dominates the countryside in which it stands and is a prominent landmark for miles around. It is special in other ways, brooding as it does over some of England's finest scenery, guarding the roads from Lancashire into Yorkshire.

It is a countryside steeped in legend and history. A land that has produced one of England's most thrilling tales, as wild and forbidding as the hill's bleak moorland summit—the story of the Witches of Pendle.

The Pendle Witches are famous throughout Britain, their story has travelled the world. Yet it is not only their incident-packed lives and deaths which have brought them this renown. Much of the credit must go to a humble court clerk, Thomas Potts, who saw in the transcripts of their trial the makings of a best-seller.

From his book "The Wonderfull Discoverie of Witches in the Countie, of Lancaster", which was published in 1613, have emerged a flood of novels, pamphlets, poems—and plays even, each adding their own embellishments to the witches' tale until the true story has become almost lost in a tangle of legends, like some ancient building overgrown by ivy. Only relatively recently has the long-awaited process of "ivy stripping" begun, laying bare just a few jumbled stones which the historian must struggle to interpret. What follows is my reconstruction.

Richard Catlow.

Left: Proud Pendle dominates the surrounding countryside.

Demdike and Chattox - Satan's consorts

The story has no clear-cut beginning, but as good a time as any is in 1603 when His Royal Highness King James VI of Scotland became King James I of England.

As the new sovereign travelled south to meet his rejoicing subjects he announced the customary pardon to all offenders. He made one exception ... those who practised witchcraft.

For James, who had written a book on how to recognise and deal with witches, did not share the traditional mixture of scepticism and tolerance on this subject.

To the average Englishman witches could be good or bad, frightening or even laughable. To James they were abhorrent creatures who had made a pact with Satan.

With a King holding such views the door was open for the intolerant, the superstitious or the unscrupulous. It was a time when an over-zealous magistrate could make his name by seeking out practitioners of the black art.

At Read Hall, between Padiham and Whalley, lived one such magistrate—Roger Nowell.

Confrontation

Nearby, in the wild slopes of Pendleside, lived two peasant families divided by hate and held in fear or respect by many of their neighbours; families who claimed to possess supernatural powers.

The stage was set for a confrontation of epic proportions.

Both families were led by old women—Old Demdike, properly named Elizabeth Southern, and Anne Whittle, alias Chattox. Tradition and the novelist have built up Demdike into the more fearsome of the two—a grim old matriarch ruling her obnoxious brood.

But her rival Chattox wielded the most power. She was acknowledged as the best maker of the clay images witches use to work their evil magic, and many of Demdike's family clearly feared her.

The two families

Demdike, a woman of about 80, halt and almost blind, lived with her widowed daughter Elizabeth Device and her three children: Alizon, a girl with what seems to have been a likeable touch of honesty; James, who was half-witted and prone to illness; and Jennet, the youngest yet most mischievous.

Chattox, another widow, lived with her daughters, Elizabeth or Bessie, and Anne. Another member of the family was Anne's husband Thomas Redfearn, a well-meaning man who, if he could not put a stop to the darker activities of the family, wisely kept out of them.

Some years before, the quarrel between the families had come out into the open when Malkin Tower, the home of the Demdikes, was broken into and some clothing and a large quantity of oatmeal stolen.

The following Sunday Alizon saw Bessie Chattox wearing a cap, one of the items which had been stolen. She rushed back to tell her family, who had to decide what measures to take.

The Demdikes of the story books would have plotted some black magic revenge, around cauldrons bubbling with strange ingredients. The real Demdikes, then led by Elizabeth's husband John Device, yielded to expediency.

John, probably afraid that his family might suffer further, arranged with Chattox to pay her a yearly tribute of meal if she would do no more harm. After some years the tribute was not paid; perhaps the family had fallen on harder times or were becoming less afraid. Whatever the reason, John died, blaming Chattox on his deathbed.

After his death the Demdikes were reduced to the life of beggars. It must have been commonplace to see the almost blind Old Mother Demdike being led along the twisting lanes by her granddaughter Alizon in the quest for alms.

Cursed

Perhaps those alms were more forthcoming as the Pendle area became filled with vague rumours of the alleged misdeeds of both the Demdikes and the Chattoxes. The rumours took fantastic forms as rumours will when their is little or no evidence to tie them to reality, but two stories were often repeated and more widely believed.

In the late 1590s, near Christmas time, Christopher Nutter, who farmed the lands around the imposing Greenhead Farm, was travelling home from Burnley with his sons Robert and John. Robert was feeling ill and attributed his sickness to the evil influence of Chattox and Anne Redfearn who lived on the Nutters' land.

His father never asked why these women should wish his son evil but Chattox was later to give plenty of justification. Robert

The family trees of the two main witch families

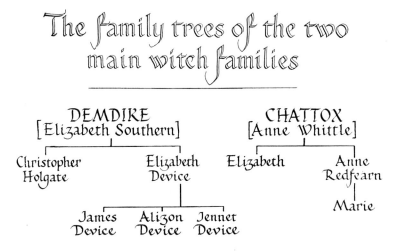

```
        DEMDIKE                         CHATTOX
   [Elizabeth Southern]             [Anne Whittle]

Christopher      Elizabeth       Elizabeth        Anne
Holgate          Device                           Redfearn

                                                    │
         James   Alizon   Jennet                   Marie
         Device  Device   Device
```

had tried to seduce Anne—who must obviously have been good looking for an alleged witch—and, when repulsed, had vowed to be revenged by banishing the family from its home.

Robert was a retainer for Sir Richard Shuttleworth of Gawthorpe Hall and had to leave for a tour of duty in the marches of North Wales. He never came back. He died in Cheshire, accusing Chattox and Anne to the end.

About a decade later Demdike's daughter Elizabeth did some work for the local miller, Richard Baldwin of Wheathead. Millers have a traditional reputation for meanness, so Elizabeth may have been quite justified in thinking herself underpaid for the task. But whether it was this or greed she sent her mother to the mill, on the banks of Pendle Water, to ask Baldwin for more money.

Old Demdike, led as usual by Alizon, could not have been expecting a favourable reception, and she did not get one. "Get off my ground, whores and witches! I will burn the one of you and hang the other!" shouted Baldwin as they approached.

It is easy to imagine Demdike replying with a curse. A curse that might have been soon forgotten had not the miller's young

daughter become ill and slowly died—not an unusual happening in those days of primitive medicine and sanitation.

The road from Colne

No action was taken on either incident. But the stories and others like them were not forgotten. The Demdikes and the Chattoxes were sitting on a powder keg. It needed only a spark to set it alight. That spark came on March 18th, 1612, when Alizon Device was returning home after a day's begging near Colne. She was alone: perhaps Old Demdike had not been feeling well enough to make the trip.

Alizon met an old pedlar, John Law of Halifax; one of those travelling salesmen who supplied the few luxuries people in those days could afford. She asked him for some pins, but he refused. In her anger she cursed him. They had hardly parted when he fell to the ground. A modern doctor would probably have diagnosed a stroke. In those days they had an uglier word ... witchcraft.

Law was carried to a nearby inn and a letter sent to his son Abraham, urging him to come at once. Abraham saw his father, who was now recovering, and after hearing his story went in search of Alizon. He found the girl and brought her to his father's bedside, where the old man charged her with bewitching him.

Confession

Alizon, probably overwhelmed by it all and brought up with a grudging belief in her family's powers, confessed and begged forgiveness. It was not forthcoming. The next day, March 30th, she was hauled before Roger Nowell at Read Hall, with her mother Elizabeth and brother James.

Confessing to the magistrate that she had lamed the pedlar, Alizon described in elaborate detail what had happened. How she had asked for the pins and been refused, upon which a black dog came up to her and spoke. The creature had asked what she would like it to do to Law, and Alizon had replied "Lame him". Almost immediately the pedlar had fallen to the floor. She had watched whilst he was taken into the alehouse, and then carried on with her begging.

Nowell must have wondered what sort of family the girl had come from to talk in such a way. He did not have to wonder very long, for Alizon went on to describe in some detail her family's involvement in witchcraft.

She told the magistrate that when she was out begging, Old Demdike had frequently asked her to let a familiar demon come to her. If she let it suck some part of her body, it would work magic on her behalf.

Alizon said that she had rejected this advice for quite some time, but had eventually agreed. The black dog had become her familiar.

This pressuring of young Alizon must have marked out Old Demdike, in Nowell's mind, as the source of the trouble. He asked for some accounts of her witchcraft.

Alizon, who seems to have set no limit at what she would say, readily complied. She described how Old Demdike had unsuccessfully tried to cure a sick cow belonging to John Nutter of Bull Hole Farm, how the old woman had managed to turn milk into butter without even rising from her bed, and how she had killed the daughter of the miller, Richard Baldwin.

Accusation

If Alizon's first statements were prompted by a desire to clear her conscience, her next were more probably motivated by malice and her family's feud. She described how Chattox had quarelled with a Higham man, John Moore. Moore had accused her of turning his ale sour and she had responded by bewitching his son John to death. Alizon even claimed to have seen Chattox making a clay image of the child with which to work her evil.

Alizon went on to recall the day, about two years previously, when she had been in the house of a man called Anthony Nutter, talking to his daughter Anne. Chattox had seen them, accused them of laughing at her, and threatened to be revenged. Within a few weeks Anne had died.

Pendle farmer Hugh Moore had also fallen foul of Chattox. He died after accusing her of bewitching his cattle. John Nutter, mentioned previously of Bull Hole Farm, had one of his cows charmed to death after quarrelling with Chattox's daughter Bessie.

Evidence

Alizon's statements were carefully written down as evidence. But it is hard to imagine that this and similar statements taken later could have been gained merely by simple questioning. Nowell must have used some sort of persuasion.

Top: Greenhead Farm, the home of Robert and Christopher Nutter.   *Bottom: Read Hall, Nowell's home, rebuilt in the early 19th century.*

In continental Europe and even Scotland at that time the persuasion would have been torture. But torture was not allowed under English Law and Nowell would have been unlikely to flout the conventions of his class and calling. The most potent weapon he could have used was a promise of mercy or leniency, backed up by a claim that he already knew the facts and only wanted them confirming from Alizon's own mouth.

Indeed Nowell must have been well aware of much of what he had been told, having heard these stories whispered by his superstitious tenantry. But if he had thought them too unbelievable to investigate then, why was he taking them so seriously now? Did he see them as a way in which a humble country magistrate could make his mark in Jacobean England? We shall never know if Nowell's proceedings were so motivated, or whether he was merely trying to do his duty in what must have been very confusing circumstances.

In the event he detained Alizon, who was guilty on her own evidence, and let the others go. On April 2nd he ordered Demdike, Chattox and Anne Redfearn, who had been singled out in Alizon's statement, to meet him at Fence—the meeting place for most Pendle Forest business.

Demdike, who had been incriminated by her own granddaughter readily made a full confession. She described how her familiar demon, a boy half brown and half black, had appeared to her many years ago in a quarry near Newchurch. She also admitted responsibility for the death of Baldwin's child.

She went on to repeat the story of how Chattox and Anne Redfearn, together with two Burnley witches—Jane Boothman and Widow Loomeshaw—had bewitched Robert Nutter to death. Chattox, perhaps overawed and quite probably believing herself responsible for the deaths, agreed.

Nowell detained Demdike, Chattox and Anne Redfearn, and sent them to stand trial with Alizon at the forthcoming assizes. Pendle must have been buzzing with the news, unaware that even more sensational things were about to happen. The Pendle Witches were about to explode onto the pages of history.

With four notorious witches safely imprisoned at Lancaster Castle, Nowell must have been feeling very pleased with himself as he relaxed at Read Hall. But his euphoria was short-lived. Out of Pendleside came even worse rumours of witchcraft and evil-doing than had ever come before.

Nowell commanded Henry Hargreaves, the forest constable, to make inquiries, and this stout-hearted yeoman visited the Demdikes' home at Malkin Tower. With the help of the half-witted James Device he unearthed some human teeth, stolen from graves at Newchurch, and a clay image. He also heard that on Good Friday there had been a great meeting of witches at the house.

On April 27th, Nowell, who was joined by fellow magistrate Nicholas Bannister of Altham, sent for James, nine-year-old Jennet and their mother Elizabeth Device. They were questioned and seemingly with the same frankness shown by Alizon, Jennet gave the magistrates another almost incredible statement.

She described how 20 witches had gathered at the Malkin Tower that fateful evening, to feast on stolen mutton and plot murder. She named six of those who had been there and James obligingly added several more.

They were: Elizabeth Device; Demdike's son Christopher Holgate; Elizabeth his wife; Jennet Hargreaves, of Under Pendle; Grace Hay, of Padiham; Christopher and Elizabeth Hargreaves of Thorneyholme; John Bulcock and his mother Jane, of Moss End Farm, Newchurch; Alice Gray, of Colne; Katherine Hewitt (alias Mouldheels), also of Colne; Ann Cronkshaw, of Marsden; Jennet Preston, of Gisburn; and the enigmatic Alice Nutter, of Roughlee.

The most surprising name on the list was that of Alice Nutter. Why should this well-to-do gentlewoman associate with what was little more than a group of peasants? Was she really a witch, or was one of her accusers motivated by some hidden malice? It seems we shall never know.

To make matters worse for Alice, Elizabeth Device confessed that the two of them had bewitched a man called Henry Mytton to death for refusing to give Old Demdike a penny. Though why a person of Mistress Nutter's means should conspire in this is never explained.

The first piece of business at the gathering concerned Jennet Preston of Gisburn, who had recently been acquitted on a charge

Top left: Bull Hole Farm where Demdike failed to cure a sick cow.

Bottom left: Ashlar House at Fence was there when Nowell interviewed the witches.

Top right : Roughlee Hall where Alice Nutter lived.

Bottom right: Lancaster Castle where the witches were imprisoned and tried.

of witchcraft at York, and wanted help to wreak vengeance on the man who had denounced her.

But the main item on the witches' agenda was a plot to blow up Lancaster Castle, kill the governor and rescue the women held there. Quite an undertaking, as anyone who has seen the castle's mighty walls will agree.

James, who seems to have been even more explicit than his sister Alizon, told Nowell that he was responsible for two deaths. He had killed Anne Towneley, of Carr Hall, near Nelson, when she had accused him and his mother of stealing peat turves for their fire. James said he had made a clay image of Anne and slowly allowed it to crumble. As it crumbled she had fallen ill and died.

The other person to suffer was John Duckworth of Laund, who had promised James an old shirt and then withdrawn his offer. James had touched Duckworth, thus gaining power over him, and with the help of his familiar demon, a dog named Dandie, Duckworth had been killed.

James also told Nowell how his mother, Elizabeth, had killed a local farmer, John Robinson, alias Swyer, of Barley, again using a clay image. Robinson had unwisely accused Elizabeth of having a bastard child. Elizabeth admitted this murder and added that she had killed the farmer's brother James, though whether this was for the same offence we aren't told.

Packed off to Lancaster

Nowell acted quickly. He detained Elizabeth and James and packed them off to Lancaster with the Bulcocks, Katherine Hewitt and Alice Gray. No mention is made of the other people at the Malkin Tower meeting, probably they had fled the area until it was safe to return.

At Lancaster the castle governor, Thomas Covell, an influential man who was Coroner for the County and several times Mayor of Lancaster, examined Chattox and James Device. By this time, probably due to her age, the journey and conditions in the medieval fortress, Demdike was a dying woman. She was never to stand trial.

Perhaps because of Demdike's condition Chattox significantly changed her story, blaming Demdike for converting her to witchcraft. The conversion, never mentioned or even hinted at earlier, had taken place, according to Chattox, at the Malkin Tower,

Left: Memorial brass to the prison govenor, Thomas Covell.

where the two women had been served a meal by their demon familiars. At this meal Demdike had confessed to being responsible for the death of Richard Assheton, of Downham, and to helping in the killing of Robert Nutter.

Chattox may have thought that by assuming less prominence in the dark events of Pendleside she increased her chances of mercy. But all she achieved was to establish her rival as the chief of the Pendle Witches: a myth that still holds sway today.

The defendants were joined by suspects from other parts of the county, among them Margaret Pearson, of Padiham, accused of bewitching a neighbour's horse; Isobel Roby, of Windle, near St. Helens; and seven people who were to become known as the Samlesbury Witches.

The first trials

On Monday, August 17th, the assizes opened before Judges Sir Edward Bromley and Sir James Altham. In spite of the many complex cases with which the judges had to deal the trials were not to last very long.

First in the dock was Chattox. Old and bent, her lips constantly chattering—a fact which had probably given rise to her nickname—a corruption of "Chatterbox"—she was charged with the killing of Robert Nutter, of Greenhead, to which she pleaded not guilty. There was no mention of the other charges laid at her door by Alizon in the statement to Nowell.

The evidence against Chattox was read out. It was too much for her, and she broke down in tears, admitted all, and asked for mercy to be shown to her daughter Anne Redfearn.

Elizabeth Device was next to appear. Described as being an extremely ugly woman, she must have looked like everyone's idea of a witch. She was charged with murdering three people by witchcraft; John Robinson, of Barley, and his brother James, and —with her mother and Alice Nutter—Henry Mytton, of Roughlee. She had already admitted these offences to Nowell and Bannister, but she fiercely denied them in the packed courthouse.

It seems unlikely that Elizabeth could have convinced the court of her innocence, but Nowell, who was prosecuting, was taking no chances. He produced a star witness in Elizabeth's own daughter, young Jennet Device. When Elizabeth saw Jennet she cursed and shouted at her, and she had to be led away still calling out violently.

Star witness

Jennet was stood on a table to enable her audience to get a better look at her. She said that she had often seen her mother's familiar demon, a brown dog named Ball, which had helped in the three killings. Her evidence was followed by written testimony from her brother James, who named Elizabeth as the chief mover behind the Good Friday meeting at Malkin Tower.

Hearing her own daughter give evidence against her must have been too much for Elizabeth. She returned to the courtroom, quietly pleaded guilty and asked for mercy.

Next in the dock was her son James who, weak by nature, had been reduced to a pitiable state by his time in gaol. He had to be virtually dragged into court and supported in the dock. He was charged with murdering Anne, wife of Henry Towneley of Carr Hall, and John Duckworth of Laund.

Anne Towneley's husband was called, but Potts did not record his evidence, virtually the only evidence from anyone of any standing in society. Was his note-taking perhaps too slow to be accurate? Did he fear to take the liberties with the words of a gentleman that he might have taken with those of humbler station? If so one wonders how accurate is the evidence that he did record.

James pleaded guilty to both killings, but he was further charged with bewitching to death John Hargreaves of Goldshawbooth and Blaze Hargreaves of Higham. He denied the charges, but once again young Jennet was brought back into the court, and once again her evidence secured conviction.

Anne Redfearn was next to appear. She was found not guilty of the murder of Robert Nutter. But a second charge, of murdering Nutter's father Christopher, was found to be proven, in spite of a singular lack of evidence and the entreaties of old Chattox. From the first time she was interviewed until her death Anne maintained her innocence.

A hush must have fallen over the assembly as the name of Alice Nutter was read out. A gentlewoman, of vastly different station to the other accused, she seems to have been deserted by her well-connected family. Perhaps their failure to stand by her or to pull any strings on her behalf implied guilt; certainly there was nothing more concrete than the word of a fanciful child, and a dull-witted man.

Alice was accused with taking part in the murder of Henry Mytton, the man who had refused to give Old Demdike a penny.

The court heard written submissions on this from James and Jennet, who also mentioned that Mistress Nutter had been present at the Good Friday meeting.

The judges decided to hold an identity parade and Alice and a group of other women were assembled. But Jennet went unhesitatingly towards Alice, took her hand and reiterated the claim that she had been at the Malkin Tower on Good Friday. Alice Nutter maintained her innocence, but was found guilty.

Katherine Hewitt, who bore the colourful name of Mouldheels, was charged with the murder of a Colne child, Anne Foulds, and was said to be in the process of bewitching another youngster, the child of Michael Hartley, to death. The evidence against her was in statements supplied by Elizabeth and James Device, but Katherine was also picked out at an identity parade by Jennet and accused of being at the Malkin Tower meeting. She too pleaded not guilty, but the case against her was found to be proved.

But mystery surrounds Alice Gray, the other Colne woman, who was tried on the same charges and the same evidence, yet acquitted. Potts leaves us no account to explain why this happened.

Next to appear were John Bulcock, his mother Jane and Alizon Device, the girl whose begging of pins had started the whole affair. The Bulcocks lived at Moss End Farm, near Newchurch, and were accused of turning Jennet Deane, of Newfield Edge, near Barnoldswick, gradually mad. They were picked out at yet another identity parade by Jennet, who, with her usual flair, added that at the Good Friday meeting John had turned the spit on which the stolen mutton had been roasted. A statement from James Device was read out to show that the couple had indeed turned Jennet Deane mad, and the Bulcocks were found guilty, in spite of loud protestations of innocence.

Alizon stood trial accused of laming John Law that fateful day in Colne. Confronting her in court was the pedlar himself, still in a very distressed condition, according to Potts. The sight was too much for Alizon, who fainted, confessing her guilt when she was eventually revived.

The sight of the afflicted pedlar must have moved the court also, for the judges promised that something would be done to provide for him. (To this day a Burnley Family named Law still avoid using the name John for their children.)

Sentenced to death

Now the witches were brought back to hear their sentences. After urging those who had not already done so to confess their sins and ask God's forgiveness the judge ordered them to be taken and hanged.

In passing sentence Sir Edward Bromley said:

"You of all people have the least cause of complaint; since on the trial for your lives there hath been much care and pains taken; and what persons of your nature and condition were ever arraigned and tried with so much solemnity? The court hath had great care to receive nothing in evidence against you but matter of fact. As you stand simply—your offences and bloody practices not considered—your fate would rather move compassion than exasperate any man; for whom would not be moved by the ruin of so many poor creatures at one time, as in appearance simple and of little understanding? But the blood of these innocent children and others his Majesty's subjects whom cruelly and barbarously you have murdered and cut off, cries unto the Lord for vengeance. It is impossible that you, who are stained with so much innocent blood, should either prosper or continue in this world or receive reward in the next."

If this was a case conducted with undue care, and the evidence was matter of fact, one wonders what a careless case relying on poorer evidence was like. But, so greatly have times changed, that it seems likely that Sir Edward's words were, however unlikely it may seem now, sincerely meant.

Hangings in those days, and for many years after, were a public spectacle, a holiday outing. It is easy to imagine the huge crowds that must have gathered on Thursday, August 20th, to see the witches taken from the castle dungeons to the gallows some distance away. One can almost hear the mighty cheer that went up as the hangman completed his task and good, law-abiding, citizens felt that they could go safely about their occasions.

One wonders what happened to young Jennet, deprived at a stroke of her family. Probably friends or relations took her in; we don't know. What we do know is that this child of Pendle was destined to step once again onto the pages of history. Just 21 years later she would return to Lancaster, this time on trial for her own life—facing charges of witchcraft.

Malkin Tower

Not the least of the mysteries surrounding the witches of Pendle is the question: "Where did they live"? Every schoolboy knows that Demdike lived at the Malkin Tower, but historians have differed widely over the site of this building and the origin of its appropriately evil-sounding name. Some have put it near Saddler's Farm, Newchurch, where an area is said to have been known as Malkin Fields. Others have placed it east of Blacko Tower near the present day Malkin Tower Farm. Some old masonry, forming part of a field wall, is sometimes pointed out as all that remains of the Malkin Tower.

East of Blacko Tower

The second site, although not in the heart of what is generally thought of as witch country, is within easy reach of Colne where Alizon was begging when she met the pedlar. Local historian Edgar Peel believes that a record in the registers of Colne Parish Church backs up the claim that this second location was indeed the site of Demdike's home. He says: "Elizabeth Device, Demdike's daughter, was accused of having a bastard child by a man called Sellar, an uncommon name in this area. In Colne Parish Church register about this time it mentions that there was a man named Sellar living at White Moor Farm, Blacko. In other words Elizabeth had been got into trouble by one of her neighbours."

Saddler's Farm

In favour of the Saddler's Farm site is the fact that most references to places connected with the Demdikes: Newchurch Church, Roughlee Hall, Moss End Farm and Bull Hole Farm are in the near vicinity. Demdike, who was blind and lame could not have walked far and the distance from Blacko would probably have been too great for her. Although Colne, where Alizon was begging that fateful day, is a good step further from the Saddler's Farm site, this fact could account for the girl being unaccompanied on that occasion.

Another fact in favour of the Saddler's Farm site is the reference by Potts that the sheep, which formed the main item on the menu of the Good Friday feast at Malkin Tower, had

Top left: The alternative site for Demdike's home on the hillside near Blacko.

Bottom left: Saddler's Farm where the Malkin Tower might have stood.

been stolen by James Device from a farmer at Barley. Barley is just over the hill from Saddler's Farm, the Blacko site is much further away, and a dead sheep is quite a heavy burden to carry; especially for a boy who was weakly and in poor health.

The frequent contact between the Demdikes and the Chattoxes argues that they lived fairly close together. We know that Chattox lived somewhere in Higham with West Close Booth, which is again much nearer to Saddler's Farm than Blacko. The balance of probabilities seems to favour the Saddler's Farm site, and the romantic will no doubt be glad to accept this spot, huddling as it does on the very flanks of Pendle, rather than the side of a hill some miles away.

Origin of the name

The origin of the name Malkin Tower has provoked as much discussion as its site. Suggested derivations are that Malkin means "evil folk", is the old dialect word for hare; that it comes from the word "Mawkin" meaning a slut, which would obviously be acceptable in Demdike's case; and more prosaically, that it is derived from the words malt kiln.

The word "Tower" suggests on first hearing a building of some grandeur, but this is unlikely when one considers that the Demdike's lived by begging. Very probably the family lived in some mean hovel, described as a tower by their neighbours with a typical Northern sense of humour. In much the same way as Robin Hood's giant friend was nick-named "Little John" in earlier centuries, and as humble homes today are sometimes referred to as "mansions" or "palaces".

But if research into the site of Demdike's home and the meaning of its name have led to no firm conclusions, research has at least been done.*

Much less investigation has gone into finding the home of Chattox and her family, even though she was almost undeniably the most powerful of the Pendle Witches. What records we have reiterate that Chattox lived in Higham and West Close Booth, on land owned by the Nutters of Greenhead, near to a river with the clay banks so necessary for the image making at which she was supreme.

Banks of clay

By Pendle Hall farm, near to the footbridge at the bottom of Ightenhill Lane, is a ruined building known to local tradition as the "witches cottage". Conveniently near to the River Calder and its banks of clay, could this be the site of Chattox's home?

Right: Pendle Hall Farm and the area in which Chattox may have lived.

The Yorkshire Witch

Although the Witches of Pendle, thanks to Harrison Ainsworth's novel, have become known as the Lancashire Witches, one of their number, Jennet Preston, was from Yorkshire. She lived just over the county boundary as Gisburn and because of this was tried at York, not Lancaster.

A poor woman she had been befriended by a wealthy local family, the Listers, of Westby Hall on the outskirts of Gisburn. The head of the family was Thomas Lister, who thought so well of Jennet that she was given everything she needed.

When Thomas died in 1607 his son, also called Thomas, continued to treat Jennet well. But local people believed Jennet was a witch and any losses of cattle and property were put down to her evil powers. Among those who had been suffering losses was young Thomas Lister, who turned against Jennet.

Tried and acquitted

In the Lent of 1612, just a few weeks before the other Pendle witches were arraigned, she was sent by Lister to stand trial at York for the murder of the child of a local man named Dodgson. The judge was the same Sir Edward Bromley who officiated at Lancaster. Jennet was acquitted and might have chosen to live out her life in peace. Instead, just a few days later, she was at the Malkin Tower for the Good Friday meeting, hoping to enlist support for the revenge she sought against Thomas Lister.

After James and Jennet Device had told Nowell about the gathering, word went out for Jennet Preston's arrest. She was caught and taken before her local magistrate, Thomas Heber of Marton. This time she was accused of killing Thomas Lister the Elder, her old friend who had died five years previously.

Tried again

Taken back to York, Jennet was tried this time by Judge Bromley's partner, Sir James Altham. Heber, who was prosecuting, produced several witnesses to testify against her. One of them, Anne Robinson, swore that when Lister was on his deathbed he had cried out that Jennet was responsible or his sickness. Altham does not seem to have asked why no action was taken by Lister's son at that time.

Left: The Ribblesdale Arms at Gisburn was built by one of the Lister family which led the campaign against Jennet Preston.

Yet Lister and Anne Robinson both calmly stated that when Jennet was taken to see the body it suddenly spouted fresh blood—a sign which in those days was taken as a certain indication of witchcraft.

Altham was obviously impressed by this declaration and he told the jury to take special note of it. Other evidence against Jennet had been provided by Roger Nowell, in the form of a statement by James Device that she had been at the Malkin Tower meeting. All this was judged to be sufficient; the jury found Jennet Preston guilty and she was sentenced to death, still protesting her innocence.

Her husband and family were naturally upset. They went back home complaining that Jennet had been maliciously prosecuted —indeed, persecuted—by Thomas Lister. It was in this frame of mind that they went to the trial at Lancaster, but their views were changed when they heard the ubiquitous Jennet Device describe those who had been at the Malkin Tower gathering. After reciting those names she knew, young Jennet added that also there had been a "woman from Craven". The Prestons were convinced that they had been mistaken, and went away satisfied that *their* Jennet had indeed been a witch.

The Samlesbury Witches

Appearing with the Pendle Witches were another group who have become known as the "Samlesbury Witches". They faced similar, though unrelated charges to their more famous co-defendants, and their trial also hinged on the evidence of a child witness. In this case there was a strong undercurrent of Catholicism, the outlawed faith which has always remained strong in the Ribble Valley.

Potts lists seven people who were charged, but he only records the trials of the principal characters: Jennet Bierley, Ellen Bierley and Jane Southworth. Once again there was a connection with high society, for Jane, a widow, was a daughter of Richard Sherbourne, of Stonyhurst.

Witness for the prosecution
They were charged with working magic upon Grace Sowerbutts, the 14-year-old daughter of Thomas Sowerbutts, a husbandman of Samlesbury, and had been examined by local magistrate Robert Holden on April 15th.

Grace, whom the defendants were charged with causing to waste away, was the principal witness and seems to have relished her role in much the same way as did young Jennet Device. She was also prepared to give evidence against her own family, for Jennet Bierley was her grandmother and Ellen her aunt.

Grace told the court that the former had once turned into a dog walking on its hind legs, which tried to tempt her to drown herself. Later the dog had tried to suffocate Grace by lying on top of her when she was asleep in a barn.

After this her grandmother and Ellen had tried to involve Grace in some of their evil-doing, taking her late at night to the home of Thomas Walshman at Samlesbury. They had crept into the bedroom, lifted the Walshmans' baby from its bed and taken it to the fireside, where Jennet had stuck a nail in its navel and sucked its blood.

As a result of this the baby had wasted away and died. The Bierley's waited for the burial and then, taking Grace with them, stole out at dead of night to take up the body from the grave. The body was taken back to Jennet's house, boiled and eaten, though Grace emphasised that she and her cousin Grace Bierley refused to take part in this cannibalism. After their meal the two witches had used the baby's fat to make a magic ointment for use in satanic rites.

Grace had further horrors to recite. She described how she and three other women were in the habit of going to a secluded place on the banks of the River Ribble to indulge their depravity. There they had met regularly "four black things going upright and yet not like men in the face", who carried them across the river, danced with them and abused their bodies.

The girl, obviously warming to her tale, said that she had met Jane Southworth when visiting her uncle at Hoghton. The widow had carried her into a loft where she was later found senseless. On another occasion Jane was supposed to have transported her to the top of a nearby haystack, where once again she was found insensible. After their third meeting Grace was found in a similar state, lying in a ditch.

Other witnesses added their belief that Jane was a witch, and there were several neighbours only too ready to testify to her evil ways.

Perjury

But Judge Bromley was clearly unconvinced by this mass of evidence. He asked the three accused if there was anything they wanted to say, and they begged him to ask Grace who had primed her with her testimony. The judge, stern-faced, turned to the child, who must have wilted before his gaze, and questioned her. Grace was unable to find answers to his skilful probing and at length, despairing, replied that although she had been ... "Put to a master to learne, he told her nothing of this".

The accused must have gasped with relief, for now it was clear to both judge and jury that Grace had been coached into weaving a fabric of lies. Luckily for the alleged witches, that coaching had not been good enough. But were the Pendle Witches perhaps hanged because someone had manipulated young Jennet Device better?

When Grace was further questioned it became clear that she had been taught by a Jesuit priest calling himself Thompson, who had persuaded her to make the false accusations against the three women because they were Catholics who had been converted to the Protestant faith. It later became known that the Jesuit's name was not Thompson, but Southworth, a member of the same family as Jane Southworth.

As a Jesuit, the order that had been recently founded to lead the Counter Reformation, Southworth was obviously prepared to go to any lengths to ensure that the Catholic flock remained staunch.

One also wonders if magistrate Robert Holden, who had brought the case to court, had not been over-zealous in his duties, inspired perhaps by the example of Nowell and Bannister and desiring to emulate them?

The Padiham Witch

Among the other witches to appear before the court at Lancaster was Margaret Pearson of Padiham, a small place on the fringes of Pendleside. She was tried on charges completely separate from those of the Pendle Witches, but there were plenty of witnesses to speak of the magic she had practised nearby.

Twice acquitted

The case against her was taken by Nowell's fellow magistrate Nicholas Bannister, of Altham. What makes the case so interest-

Left: These stocks at Colne would have had a familiar look to Margaret Pearson.

ing is that here was a living proof that suspected witches could and did obtain justice in England at this time, for Margaret Pearson had been tried and acquitted on charges of witchcraft twice before.

The modern reader is appalled at what seems to be the ridiculously short time which the trials of the Demdikes and Chattoxes took up, and the unsatisfactory nature of much of the evidence against them. But rough justice as this was, it's still justice of a sort, better by far than the virtually mock trials then practised in other countries, and it is worthy of record that Margaret Pearson was by no means the only person to have been acquitted on charges of witchcraft in those bigoted times.

In her first trial she had been accused of murder, in the second of bewitching a man. This time she was accused of killing a mare, the property of a Padiham man named Dodgson.

Chattox again

Margaret had the misfortune to have shared a cell with the other witches, notably Chattox, who at this stage was consigned to the gallows herself and seems to have decided to take others with her. After several Padiham people had told the court they were convinced that Margaret had killed the mare, Chattox said that the woman had confessed in the cell to killing the wife and child of a man named Childer *and* to killing the mare.

Chattox described how Margaret and her familiar demon had crawled into the animal's stable through a loop-hole and sat on it until it collapsed and died. Chattox added that, in her opinion, Margaret was every bit as evil as herself.

The next witness was a Padiham woman—yet another Jennet! This time a Jennet Booth, whose fantasies would have done credit to a fairy tale. Jennet, it seems, had gone with her child to Margaret's house to card wool and, feeling hungry, had asked for something to eat. Margaret had brought a pan of milk and set it to boil. As it did so there appeared a toad inside it, which Margaret had picked up with a pair of tongs and taken outside the house.

The manifestation evidently impressed the jury for they returned a verdict of guilty. But there was to be no gallows for Margaret. She was condemned instead to stand in the pillory for six hours at the markets of Lancaster, Padiham, Whalley and Clitheroe. Above her head a paper would record her crimes ... and no doubt ensure a good pelting from the townsfolk. After this she was to spend a year in gaol.

The Witch of Windle

Isobel Roby of Windle was the last prisoner to be tried. She was not connected with the other witches, but her appearance on charges of witchcraft must have whetted the appetite of court clerk Potts in anticipation of yet another sensation.

Isobel had been examined and charged by her local lord of the manor and magistrate, Sir Thomas Gerard, on July 12th. On that day several neighbours had gone before him to complain about Isobel's alleged misdeeds.

Aches and pains

Peter Chadwick, of Windle, told Sir Thomas that she had been displeased when he had married. He had called her a witch and for some time after both he and a friend, Thomas Lyon, had suffered from aching bones. Later she had quarrelled with Chadwick's wife, after which the wife had suffered from a pain in the neck.

Chadwick had got the local healer, James a Glover, to cure them. But it had been long and painful work. Once again it became clear that this was a family quarrel. For Isobel turns out to be the godmother of Chadwick's wife. But there were other witnesses as well.

Jane, the wife of Francis Wilkinson of Windle, said that she had been ill after refusing to give Isobel some milk. Another Windle woman, Margaret Lyon, said that she had heard Isobel bragging about her curse on Peter Chadwick; adding that Chadwick was frightened of the witch. Margaret Parr, also of Windle, had also heard Isobel claim to have bewitched Jane Wilkinson.

Hanged like the rest

The net had tightened, and Isobel seems to have been unable to find a loophole. The jury had little hesitation in pronouncing her guilty of "Fellonie by witchcraft", and the death sentence was passed. She was hanged with the Demdikes and the Chattoxes Unlike them she could not even have the satisfaction of earning a place in history. She was just another sad victim of ignorance, hatred and hysteria.

King James and Daemonologie

King James I of England, VI of Scotland, was one of the most intellectually gifted people ever to come to the throne. But his practice of thinking along narrow and rigid lines, and the consequences of this, earned him the title "The wisest fool in Christendom".

One of the subjects to which he gave most thought was witchcraft and this, combined with an overweening sense of his own importance, led James to think himself as the chief target for his country's witches. When stormy seas interrupted the passage of his Danish bride to Scotland, he was convinced witchcraft was responsible, and in a fit of paranoia he sought out, tried and executed victims who were tortured into making confessions of guilt.

Book on Witchcraft

James was a regular attender at witch trials; and Scotland was the scene of many more such than its more tolerant neighbour England. He noted what he saw and heard, and in 1594—nine years before he became King of England—wrote and published a book "Daemonologie", that described the practices of witches and how they could be identified.

With such an illustrious author the book could hardly fail to be a success. It became the generally accepted treatise used for reference and guidance in witch trials. Although Potts makes no mention of it, the form taken by the confessions of the Pendle Witches shows that magistrate Roger Nowell, Thomas Covell and the trial judges were all acquainted with it.

James warned in his book that witchcraft was an act of treason against the king. He said that the evidence of children, mad women and persons of bad character was acceptable in cases of this sort. "For," he asked, "who but witches can be provers and so witnesses of the doings of witches?"

Proof positive

But there were two additional pieces of evidence that could also be obtained. If a witch was stripped and searched there would be found a place on her body that was insensitive to pain. Special needles were used to search for these places, which

Left: Hoghton Tower where King James once stayed and reputably knighted a loin of beef.

were believed to be the spot where the witch's familiar demon sucked blood at intervals. Whether such a search was conducted on the Pendle Witches we do not know, but Demdike's family said that the old crone had a witch mark on the left side of her body.

Other evidence of witchcraft could be obtained by throwing the suspect into water—the age old trial by ordeal. It was believed that the water would not swallow up evil. Consequently witches floated and were then killed by due process of law, while innocents sank and ran the strong risk of drowning. There is no evidence that Pendle's witches were subjected to this judgement of the waters: probably the evidence against them was already considered ample.

James believed that all witches had made a compact with the Devil. They were usually tempted by promises of riches, power or aid in revenge, and were usually women, because women were the weaker sex. Each witch had his or her own familiar demon, often in the shape of a dog or cat, who guided them in the arts of evil. These arts could include anything from causing or curing illnesses to controlling the weather.

If a king believed all this, then it is little wonder that ordinary people could go in terror of witches, and condone and even applaud the barbaric treatment meted out to suspects. James ordered that the punishment for practitioners should be death, preferably by burning, but England continued with its traditional system of hanging.

A model confession

The confession of Margaret Johnson of Marsden (modern-day Nelson), a witch tried in 1634, has everything a good witch confession should have; the bargain with the Devil, the familiar demon, devil's marks, witches' meetings and black magic. It runs:

"That betwixt seven or eight years since, she being in her own house in Marsden in great passion and anger and discontent, and withal pressed with some want (short of money), there appeared unto her a spirit or devil in the proportion or similitude to a man, apparelled in a suit of black, tied about with silk points; who offered that if she would give him her soul he would supply all her wants and bring to her whatsoever she did need; and at her appointment would in revenge either kill or hurt whom or what she desired, were it man or beast.

"And saith that after a solicitation or two she contracted and covenanted with the said devil for her soul. And that the said

devil or spirit bade her call him by the name of Mamilian, and when she would have him to do anything for her, call in Mamilian and he would be ready to do her will. And saith that in all her talk and confidence she calleth her said devil 'Mamil my god'. She further saith that the said Mamilian, her devil did abuse and defile her body (that is sexual intercourse took place).

"And saith that she was not at the great meeting at Hoarestones, at the Forest of Pendle, upon All Saints Day, but saith she was at a second meeting the Sunday next after All Saints Day, where there was at the time between thirty and fourty witches who did all ride to the said meeting, and the end of the meeting was to consult for the hurting of men and beasts. And saith that besides their private familiars or spirits there was one great or grand devil or spirit more eminent than the rest ...

"She also saith that if a witch had but one mark, she hath but one spirit; if two then two spirits; if three yet but two spirits. And saith that their spirits usually have keeping of their bodies."

After Margaret had gone on to name those at the witches' meeting, the deposition continued:

"Good Friday is one constant day for a yearly general meeting of witches, and that on Good Friday last they had a meeting near Pendle Water. She also saith that men witches usually have women spirits and women witches men spirits. And their devil or spirit gives them notice of their meeting and tells them the place where it must be. And saith if they (the witches) desire to be in any place upon a sudden their devil or spirit will, upon a rood (or broomstick) dog or anything else, presently convey them thither; yea into any room of a man's house ...

"She also saith that the devil (when sucking) will make a pap or dug in a short time and the matter which he sucks is blood. And saith that their devils can cause foul weather and storms and so did at their meetings. She also saith that when her devil did come to suck her pap he usually came to her in the likeness of a cat, sometimes of one colour and sometimes of another. And that since this trouble (being accused and questioned) befell her, her spirit hath left her, and she never saw him since."

Margaret's story contains the basis of the fairytale witch, of black cat and broomstick. Luckily for her much had changed in the 20 years since Demdike and Chattox had been tried, and hanged for similar confessions.

Change in the law

Thanks to people like Dr. John Webster, who exposed the whole sham of witchfinding, views were to change even further. In 1735 a bill of George II repealed James's laws on witchcraft and instead prohibited "any prosecution, suit or proceeding against any person for withcraft, sorcery, enchantment or conjuration". The Age of Reason had dawned at last, but a little too late for some.

The Outbreak of 1633

In 1633 England was set alight by stories of another outbreak of witchcraft in Pendle — far worse than that of 1612. But although almost everyone nowadays knows something of Demdike and Chattox, the story of the witches of 1633 has almost been forgotten. Yet this was probably the most exciting witch story of all. In spite, or even because of its sensational details the account is usually only to be found in the appendices of modern day books.

Hallowe'en

It begins on Hallowe'en 1632, just as the cold autumn night was beginning to close in on the unlit hamlets of Pendleside. An 11-year-old boy was out searching for wild plums. He came back with what must be the "plum" witch story of all time. He claimed to have come across two greyhounds, one black the other brown. The animals came up to him fawning and he noticed that each had a shining gold collar from which trailed a lead. The dogs looked like those belonging to a neighbour, but when the owner did not appear, Edmund decided to go in hunt of hares.

At that moment a hare ran from the long grass near him and he urged the dogs to chase it. When the animals refused, Edmund tethered them to a nearby hedge and started to thrash them with his stick. As he brought down the stick on the animals' backs, the black hound was transformed before his eyes. In its place stood a neighbour, Frances Dickenson. The brown hound was also transformed, into a small boy whom Edmund did not recognise.

Edmund was terrified and tried to run, but the woman seized him and offered him a shilling if he would keep secret what he

Right: Hoarstones at Fence, where Edmund saw the witches feasting.

had seen. He refused saying; "Nay, thou art a witch." The woman reached into her pocket and produced a bridle which she placed on the small boy's head. Immediately the child was changed into a white horse, and the witch mounted it, forcing Edmund to ride beside her.

Feasting at Hoarstones

They rode to a house called Hoarstones, at Fence. There Edmund saw a great assembly of men and women feasting on meat, smoking flesh and lumps of butter, pulled down from the beams above with the aid of long ropes. Three women were poking among the beams and from them they produced three clay images pierced with thorns. Edmund knew that he had been taken to a witches' gathering.

Somehow the boy managed to escape, pursued by two of the witches. He must have been caught had not the approach of two horsemen frightened them off. Edmund hid, quivering in the undergrowth, at a place called Boggart Hole until the coast was clear. Then he rushed home to tell his father, a stone mason also called Edmund, what he had seen. But for the time being, the lad's amazing revelations went no further than the four walls of their home.

Sinister woman

Soon after New Year, 1633, Edmund happened to see one of the women who had pursued him. She was called Mrs. Loynd and was sitting in the beams of his house. Edmund called to her to come down, but the witch just vanished into thin air. Shortly after this Edmund had an even more unnerving experience when, going to bring in his father's cows, he was attacked by a boy. Edmund was having decidedly the worst of the encounter when, looking down, he saw that his adversary had a cloven hoof. He turned and ran towards a light he could see nearby, to find that it was a lantern held by the sinister Mrs. Loynd. Again he ran home to tell another amazing tale.

This time Edmund's tale went further than his father. At Padiham, on February 10th, he was interviewed by local magistrates John Starkie, of Huntroyde, and Richard Shuttleworth, of Gawthorpe Hall. The two men were faced with a tale even more fanciful than those with which Roger Nowell had been confronted. The story might well have been dismissed out of hand, except for the fact that one of the men, John Starkie, had very good reason to take tales of witchcraft very seriously indeed.

The mind of John Starkie

More than 30 years before, in 1596, John Starkie, then aged 10, his sister Ann and five others, had become possessed by demoniacal spirits, though a modern doctor would probably have diagnosed epilepsy or mass hysteria. The children were living at Cleworth Hall, near Leigh, one of the Starkies' homes. Their anxious father, Nicholas Starkie, called in a conjurer named Hartley, who, by herbal remedies and charms, managed to cure the youngsters.

Hartley stayed with the family, at their expense and to his convenience, for 18 months, when Nicholas Starkie, who must have become exasperated at the conjurer's persistence, ordered him to leave. But Hartley had hardly left the building when John Starkie started bleeding.

The conjurer was recalled. After stopping the bleeding he was invited back into the Starkies' home, and even offered a pension. But Hartley was becoming greedy. Seeing a chance to make even more from his powers he demanded a house and land of his own. When this was refused he vowed revenge. The next day the two Starkie children and five other members of the household fell into hysterical fits.

This and other events made Nicholas Starkie suspicious. He thought back to the time when, in the woods near Whalley, Hartley had drawn a magic circle and asked him to participate in mysterious rites. Eventually Hartley was brought before two magistrates, who sent him to stand trial at Lancaster Assizes, where he was charged with witchcraft, found guilty and hanged.

These proceedings must have produced a deep impression on John Starkie's mind. If any man could be excused for believing Edmund Robinson's fanciful tale, then he was that man.

Witches galore—one in particular!

Edmund was asked to name the people he had seen at Hoarstones. They were: Frances Dickenson, Mrs. Henry Priestley and her son, the widow Alice Hargreaves, Mrs. Henry Jacks and her son John, James Hargreaves of Marsden, Mrs. Miles Dicks, a Mrs. James, Mr. and Mrs. Saunders, Mrs. Loynd, Mrs. Boys of Barrowford, Mr. and Mrs. Holgate and the wife of Little Robin

Right: Gawthorpe Hall near Padiham where magistrate Richard Shuttleworth lived.

of West Close. Also named were William Device, a member of the famous witch family, and Jennet Device—though her name is spelt Davies now—the granddaughter of Old Demdike and the star witness at the earlier trials. It was ironical that she was to become the victim of a child witness herself.

There were 17 altogether who were rounded up and sent to stand trial within the precincts of Lancaster Castle. They were all found guilty and sentenced to death, but the judge ordered a stay of execution until the matter could be reported to the King at London.

Examined by doctors . . .

This time, however, there were to be no executions. James I was dead and his son Charles I, a much more tolerant sovereign, was on the throne. Charles read the report of the trial and ordered four of the women to be sent to London for closer examination. The others were to be interviewed by the Bishop of Chester.

The four were examined by numerous surgeons and midwives, among them the cream of England's scientific elite, then later by King Charles himself. Although one of the women, Margaret Johnson of Marsden, had made a full and voluntary confession with grimly detailed accounts of how she suckled the Devil, the medical team concluded that there was no evidence that the women were witches. The factor which had swayed them most was the absence of witchmarks.

. . . and by the clergy

The Bishop was told by two of the supposed witches, Frances Dickenson and 20-year-old Mary Spencer, that the Robinsons bore a grudge against their families. A witness backed Mrs. Dickenson's claim that Edmund's father had offered to withdraw the charges for payment. It was enough. The witches were all reprieved, though some had already died under the rigours of imprisonment and at least some of the remainder were to spend several more years in gaol.

Commercial gain

Meanwhile some people had already found out that there is money to be made in catering for people's interest in witchcraft. Four of the witches, including Mrs. Dickenson, were taken to London to be exhibited like wild beasts, drawing huge crowds eager to gaze on them. To many of the common people, the

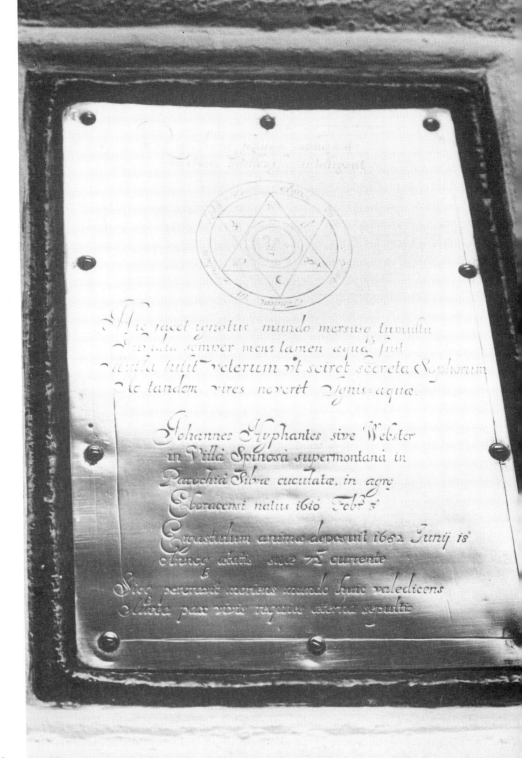

women, whatever the result of the King's investigations, were still witches. The following year their tale, dramatised as "The Late Lancashire Witches" was a big hit at the Globe Theatre.

Edmund's father and a relative were also reaping a financial reward. Every Sunday they would take the boy to a different church, where he would point out witches in the congregation. People must have lived in terror of being so denounced, and there must have been several who were quite willing to donate money or presents to make sure that they were not singled out. It seems as though the family had developed quite a lucrative trade when their career was cut short by an order for them to appear in London. The boy was segregated and severely questioned. He admitted that the whole scheme had been the concoction of his father, which he had been forced to further. The witch-finding was stopped and Edmund seems to have spent the rest of his life living quietly. We hear that in later years he was known as "Ned o' Roughs".

Debunked

But Edmund's witch saga had shown that most people, even those who had the advantages of wealth and education, were quite prepared to accept the most outlandish tales connected with witchcraft. There was one man, who notably was not. He was John Webster, headmaster of Clitheroe Grammar School and Vicar of Mytton, who, in 1677, published a book, the "Displaying of Supposed Witchcraft", which took an analytical look at Edmund's witch story, showing just how ridiculous the whole thing had been.

Webster, whose learning included surgery, metallurgy, astrology and mathematics, was a man of exceptional ability. His book and others like it had a great effect on the climate of opinion regarding witchcraft. For long years after, the common people might believe just as firmly in tales of dark deeds and black magic, but among more educated people such beliefs could never again hold the same sway.

Webster, in 1634, when curate of Kildwick, near Skipton, had come into contact with Edmund Robinson and his family, then at the height of their careers as witchfinders. The boy had come to the Sunday afternoon service and been placed on a stool so that he could survey the congregation and discover any witches among the people there. After the service Webster went round to the house where the Robinsons were staying and asked to speak to him, noting that he was in the charge of two "very unlikely persons". But these persons would not allow Webster to see Edmund. Later, in the presence of many parishioners, Webster asked the boy to tell him truthfully if he had really seen the supposed witch gathering at Hoarstones. The boy was not allowed to answer and his guardians whisked him away, leaving Webster to draw his own conclusions.

Other people were also drawing conclusions. On May 16th, 1634, Sir William Pelham wrote excitedly to Lord Conway:

"The greatest news from the country is of a huge pack of witches which are lately discovered in Lancashire, whereof, 'tis said, 19 are condemned, and that there are 60 already discovered, and yet daily are there more revealed. There are divers of them of good ability and they have done much harm. I hear it is suspected that they had a hand in raising the great storm wherein his Majesty was in so great danger at sea in Scotland."

Thankfully views like those of Sir William did not prevail. After Edmund's story had been exposed in London memory of his "discoveries" gradually faded away. But if James not Charles had been on the throne of England who is to say the story might not have had a quite different ending? That the names of Dickenson, Loynd, Johnson and Spencer might not have become as well known as those of Demdike, Chattox and Nutter.

Left: Memorial brass to Webster in Clitheroe Church is written in Latin and includes a puzzle.

The Dugdale Affair

In the late 1680s the Pendle area was once again the focus of attention as tales of foul deeds dominated local gossip, and accounts of fearful happenings spread far afield.

At the centre of events was a young man, Richard Dugdale, a gardener living with his parents at Surey (on the banks of the River Calder between Great Harwood and Whalley). At school Richard had been noted for his pranks and for his ability at acrobatics and ventriloquism, but all this seems to have been forgotten when, in 1688, his startled neighbours learned that he had become possessed by a demon.

Fits ...

Richard was 19 when violent fits began to seize him, strange fits in which it was as if he had become a devil in his bodily shape. Between attacks Richard showed a strong religious tendency and was constantly praying. He said that the only way in which he could be helped was if all the local people fasted for a day.

... and starts

Six dissenting ministers started to attend him—the Reverends Thomas Jolly, Charles Sagar, Nicholas Kershaw, Robert Waddington, Thomas Whalley and John Carrington, who held meetings at which they attempted to exorcise the demon. They were assisted on several occasions by Reverends Frankland, Pendlebury and Oliver Heywood; such was the consternation that Richard had caused.

The meetings began on May 8th, 1689 and continued, at the rate of two a month, until February next year, attracting hordes of people from far and wide.

At the first, Richard's parents explained that at Whalley rush bearing, in July, 1688, when there was much dancing and drinking, their son offered himself to the Devil if he would make him the best dancer in Lancashire. The sternly puritanical ministers must have been rubbing their hands in glee at this account of the perils which drinking and dancing led to.

Right: Altham Church where Thomas Jolly was pastor. Nicholas Bannister, one of the magistrates that Demdike appeared before, is probably buried among other members of his family to the east end of the church.

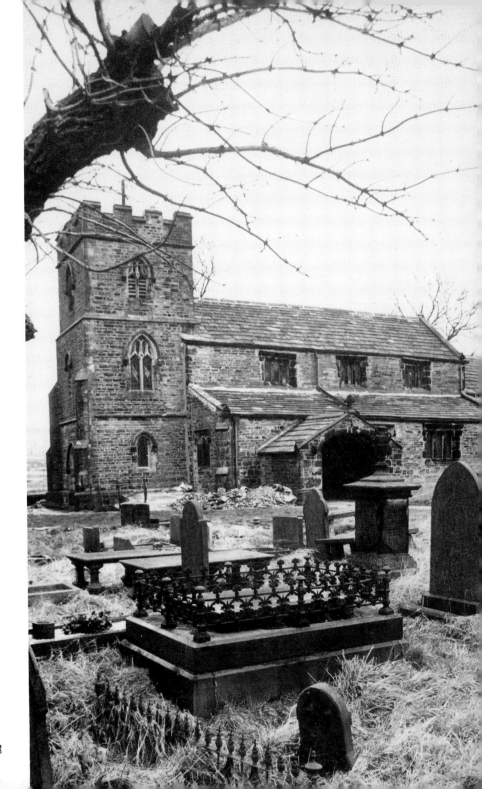

Pact with the Devil

Richard's parents added that when their son got home, after becoming extremely drunk, apparitions appeared to him and presented him with gold, fine clothing and other dainties, inviting him "To have his pleasure". In the course of the day the Devil and Richard had come to some agreement and the Devil entered him, since when he had suffered from the fits.

During these convulsions Richard's body was often hurled about violently and he would abuse his minister and shout blasphemies. Sometimes he would speak in Greek or Latin, though he had never been taught these tongues, at times his voice was almost a whisper, at others hollow and hideous. His body also changed, sometimes as heavy as lead, at others as light as a feather. His disposition was equally variable. At one moment he would be cursing his minister, at the next thanking the man for saving him from Hell.

This was not all. Richard's parents solemnly told the assembled ministers that their son could also predict when it would rain and when he would receive presents. Even more amazing was an ability to vomit large pebbles, and a queer noise in his throat, as if he was singing his psalms inwardly.

But the most prominent mark of demoniacal possession was a lump, which would swell up in his leg and travel, like a mole, up his body until it reached his chest. Here it would speak in strange utterings. The demon had also kept its bargain about Richard's dancing, wherein the boy could "Excell all that spectators had seen and all that mere mortals could perform".

The ministers did all they could to exorcise the demon, wrestling in great debates with it, and aided by the prescriptions of a local medical practitioner, Dr. Chew. But they seemed to be getting nowhere, and Richard cried out that if he was not cured before March 25th he would die. Miraculously the boy was cured with just one day to go.

A miracle exposed

Only once did his marvellous dancing powers return—when he had drunk too much. But still no-one suspected and three worthy magistrates, Lord Willoughby, Ralph Egerton and Thomas Braddyll, prepared a document recording Richard's feats.

At length someone less trusting decided to investigate, in the person of the Rev. Zachary Taylor, the Bishop of Chester's curate at Wigan. The ministers had published a pamphlet with the overblown title: "An Account of Satan's entering in and about the body of Richard Dugdale, and of Satan's removal thence through the Lord's blessing of the within mentioned ministers and people". The pamphlet was intended as a glowing tribute to the Nonconformists, but to Taylor it was a piece of troublesome meddling. He retorted with a pamphlet entitled: "The Surey imposter, being an answer to a late fanatical pamphlet".

There was a great deal of acrimony as pamphlet followed pamphlet on the subject. But the Rev. Taylor played a trump card in the person of Edward Slater, one of Dugdale's old school friends. Slater recalled the strange antics and acrobatics that Dugdale had got up to at school, and said he was convinced that the so-called possession was a fake.

Taylor lambasted the ministers for their handling of the case and even claimed that the hoax had been of their invention. This was unlikely to have been true; if the ministers had been guilty of gullibility, they were innocent of deceit. However, the affair that had promised so well for their cause had rebounded to its detriment.

Outbreak in Rossendale

Witches were always believed to wield great power where the health of farm animals was concerned. In centuries gone by, when the death of a cow could spell starvation for families struggling along at subsistence level, the bewitching of animals was a very serious matter indeed. Even to better off farmers it could be of grave concern.

Not for nothing were most stables protected by horse shoes, lucky stones or other charms. But even these time-hallowed remedies were sometimes inadequate.

About 200 years ago farmers in Rossendale were being particularly troubled by witchcraft. Cream was soured in the churn and would give no butter, cows died unaccountably in the shippons, horses were bewitched from their stables and found wandering far afield and the sheep were also affected.

Suspicion

At length suspicion came to rest on an old man, a well-known fortune teller, who lived near Newchurch-in-Rossendale. The farmers decided to get rid of him by performing a bit of magic themselves.

It was a cold evening in Autumn when they began their rites for "killing the witch". The farmers met at the house of one of their number, took a live cock chicken, stuck it full of pins and burned it alive, at the same time repeating magical rhymes. An oatmeal cake, mixed with the urine of some of the affected animals, was also prepared. The name of the witch was written on top of it and the cake was then burned.

An account of the incident describes what happens next:

"The wind suddenly rose to a tempest and threatened the destruction of the house. Dreadful moanings, as of someone in intense agony, were heard without, whilst a sense of horror prevailed upon all within."

At the mercy of the elements

When the storm reached its peak there was a knock on the farmhouse door, and the voice of the old witch could be heard pleading to be let in. Luckily the farmers had been warned, by the wise man they had consulted, that this would happen and

Right: Newchurch-in-Rossendale, once the home of a notorious wizard.

been told that on no account must they let the witch inside, for once he had gained access to the room his powers would recover. So the farmers hardened their hearts and made no answer as the knocking continued. The old man returned home and within a week was dead. One wonders whether this was the effect of the spell or being exposed to the Winter storm.

As a whole, hard-headed Rossendalians seem to have had a way of dealing with witches that their cousins in Pendleside would have done well to learn.

A man, living more than 150 years ago, and suffering from the evil influence of a notorious witch, went to see a famous witch doctor and fortune teller at Wardle, near Whitworth. The doctor gave him a small packet containing some unknown mixture, with instructions to hold it over the fire in a glazed earthenware pot about the hour of midnight. He cautioned him, however, to beware of allowing the mixture to drop into the fire, for this would cause the witch to burn to death.

At the time stipulated, the man, having first carefully bolted the door, took the mixture and did as was directed. Very soon an unearthly groan was heard from outside, as if coming from someone in great distress. This so terrified the man that he allowed the dish and its contents to drop from his hand into the fire. The mixture exploded with such a bang that all the neighbours were wakened by the noise. Next morning the witch was found to be dead, lying under her own bed with her right arm burnt almost to a cinder.

The Trawden Crones

Trawden, just a mile or so to the east of Colne, is another place that has associations with witches. Last century Old John o' Absalom's was prepared to swear that he had seen more than enough of these evil creatures and their doings.

He told neighbours that one day he had seen calves running up and down the walls of the cattle shed and cattle turned round in their stalls through the power of witchcraft.

Old John's son, a very resourceful youth, was also troubled by witches: one was even in the habit of coming to his room at night. So one evening the lad concealed a pitchfork beneath his bed clothes, and feigned sleep when he heard the creak of the floorboards as the crone came upstairs.

Dissolved into nothing

He waited until she had closed the door behind her, then flinging back the bedclothes, he threw the pitchfork, pinning the witch to the bedroom door. He laughed and laughed at the old woman, and defied her to escape. But the laughter died in his mouth as he saw her dissolve between the tines and disappear slowly through the keyhole.

Another Trawden witch, and they seem to have been a very unfortunate crew, had an even worse experience.

Cause and effect

It began when a group of youths decided to mistreat a sinister black cat that was always lurking in the shadows. Catching the beast, they tied its legs with string, turning it into a sort of furry black ball. They threw it into the air, wondering if it would bounce when it hit the ground. But, just as the animal was about to crash down, it vanished in a flash. A short while later it was learned that an old woman, who was confined to her bed with illness, had been found with a broken leg. Her cat was missing. This was proof enough for the superstitious villagers that the lads had discovered a witch.

The Todmorden Doe

Just over the county boundary from Burnley, indeed it was formerly part of Lancashire and still has a cricket team playing in the Lancashire League, lies Todmorden. In the 17th century it was the home of one of the area's most aristocratic witches, Lady Sybil of Bernshaw Tower.

Lady Sybil was a romantic who liked nothing better than to wander through the wooded glens of the magnificent Cliviger Gorge, especially near to the jagged rocks of Eagle Crag. But although she would spend most of her time hereabouts, Lady Sybil still envied the way in which the animals and birds could become almost part of the scenery. So much in fact that she became a witch, just so that she could wander through her favourite haunts in the shape of a white doe.

Lady Sybil spent even more of her time in the country now and had little time for the legion of admirers that her beauty attracted. Foremost among these was Sir William Towneley, of Hapton Tower near Burnley, who was driven almost to distraction by the lady's mysterious habits. Eventually he decided to consult a local wise woman.

Hunted down

The sayer told him to go hunting in the Cliviger Gorge. Sir William followed this advice and found a beautiful white doe, which he chased far and wide over the surrounding countryside. Every time he thought he had caught the creature it would slip from his grasp, so great was its knowledge of secret paths and hidden tracks. But eventually the animal tired, and near Eagle Crag Sir William caught it.

In triumph he bore it back to Hapton Tower and locked it securely away. In the morning when he went down to look at it, the white doe had vanished. In its place was the Lady Sybil.

The couple were married, but Lady Sybil's infatuation with the countryside continued. She would turn herself into a cat to go exploring.

But one exploration turned to disaster when she had a paw sliced off by a spiteful man. When she awoke in the morning Lady Sybil looked down to find her hand missing, the one bearing the signet ring which meant so much to her husband.

Using her strongest magic she managed to restore the hand, but the effort was so much for her that she was aged instantaneously and soon died. But legend has it that the white doe, and a spectral huntsman and his hound, can still be seen at night near Eagle Crag.

Tam o' Shanter

The story of the famous Robert Burns' character Tam o' Shanter, who was frightened out of a drunken stupour when he came across a gathering of witches, is well known. Less well known is a legend which records a similar incident at the now-ruined Netherwood Farm, on the lane leading from Burnley to Extwistle Hall.

A countryman on his way to Roggerham, a district near Worsthorne, saw a light shining through a loop hole of a barn at Netherwood, and unable to resist the temptation peeped through into the building. Terror-struck he saw a witches' ceremony in full swing, with naked bodies performing fantastic rites. "Lord Save us," he cried in his alarm, and the witches,

Left: The wild scenery of Cliviger Gorge where the white doe is said to roam.

Right: Towneley Hall, for many years the home of the staunchly Catholic Towneleys

unable to bear the sound of the Holy name, disappeared into darkness. Frightful forms mounted on broomsticks brushed past him in the night. It is hardly surprising that the simple country-man vanished almost equally quickly.

Religious Persecution

Beneath the tempestuous surface of the tales of Lancashire's witches runs an undercurrent of Roman Catholicism. Pendle and the Ribble Valley always have been and still are centres of Catholicism. But in the early 17th century the Catholic faith was banned, and there were severe punishments for its prac-titioners. The Catholic gentry, like the Towneleys at Towneley Hall, Burnley, continued their religion in the secrecy of their own homes and private chapels. Priest holes were built to pro-vide a refuge for the family's own preacher; younger sons were sent to study abroad and train as priests and missionaries.

But for humbler folk, unable to afford the fines for non-attendance at the established church, with no big houses to conceal their activities and no private priest to conceal, the problems of continuing to practise their faith were immense. It is only too likely that their clandestine gatherings were held at night in lonely places, in fact just the sort of places where witches were supposed to meet.

Were covens living churches?

Many of the witch names, like Nutter and Southworth, figure prominently in the Catholic role of honour during those oppressed days. Is it possible that the witches were really Catholics and that their covens were living churches? If this was so and the Malkin Tower was really a Catholic meeting place, then rumours of dark deeds and terror would be a very useful front for their gatherings, deterring all but the most determined investigation.

It is possible that Demdike and Chattox may have secretly practised the old Celtic religion, handed down from parent to child over the generations. Certainly remote Pendle Forest was just the sort of place where such practices might have survived. Although Christianity had long been the established religion, old customs died hard, and in the days when few people could read or write folk memory was still very strong.

Alice Nutter

An old Catholic belief says that Alice Nutter was really a Catholic, and that on the Good Friday that the witches met at Malkin Tower she had been to a Catholic ceremony. When accused of witchcraft she had not produced any evidence against the charge, because to do so was to put her fellow Catholics in danger. This would explain why her family made no effort to save her at the trial, in spite of their wealth and influence.

It is possible that Alice, was as the story paints her, a brave martyr. But when the penalty for witchcraft was certain death and a Catholic was likely to face only a hefty fine, it seems to be carrying courage too far.

History—ancient and modern

The history books tell us that witch trials had come to an end by the early 18th century. But, while witchcraft has not been a crime for many years now, the books are not quite right. Exactly 100 years ago two Pendleside witches stood before a magistrate at Colne. Their case was never published, because the magistrate ordered the two reporters present to put nothing in their 'papers on pain of his severe displeasure. Explaining his stance he is reputed to have said:

"This is the sort of thing that London 'papers would report at length if they could but learn of it, making game of us as a lot of ignorant and superstitious chawbacons, with not an idea in our heads beyond weft and twist". But, thankfully, a diary record of this trial has survived.

Esther "S" of Sabden—herself, writes the diarist, well known for her spells—was charged with assaulting a very old woman called Mary "R" of Narrowgates, near Barley, on Monday, January 4th, 1875. Esther was alleged to have stabbed Mary in the face with a corking pin, exclaiming as she did so: "Now I've drawn thy blood I can sleep o' nights", believing no doubt in the old proverb "Draw blood from a witch and she cannot harm you".

Hag ridden

Esther told the court that Mary had been "Hag-riding" her husband and herself for two years or more, and accused her of being a witch. Hag-riding, she explained, meant sending dreams which troubled them in their sleep. The magistrate, even though he "Could not believe in spells and such-like in the enlightened 19th century", was convinced that Esther had been acting in good faith and accordingly fined her only a shilling.

The diarist records:

"The common people still believe in witches and their spells, in spite of the ridicule with which persons who profess to be of superior education regard such things. For my part I believe in witchcraft also. I have seen too much of it to doubt its reality".

Still practised

There was indeed plenty of evidence that the morbid craft was still being practised in the Pendle area last century, though newspapers and books, not wishing to foster what was believed to be superstitious nonsense, generally chose to ignore its existence. A chairman of the Burnley Literary and Scientific Society told members he had found a bottle full of pins, buried in the churchyard at Newchurch. In his view they had been put there to work some evil.

A book of Lancashire Folk Lore of the time records that a woman living near Burnley had such a reputation for bewitching farmers' cattle that none of her neighbours dared to offend her.

It records:

"If in some thoughtless moment anyone spoke slightingly either of her or her powers, a corresponding penalty was threatened as soon as it reached her ears. The loss of cattle, personal health, or a general run of 'bad luck' soon led the offending party to think seriously of making peace with this powerful tormentor".

When age caught up with the old crone and she knew that she was dying, she summoned a friend to her bedside. Here, it is said, the friend received the witch's last breath into her mouth and with it the familiar spirit. The book records:

"The dreaded woman thus ceased to exist, but her powers for good or evil were transferred to her companion, and on passing along the road from Burnley to Blackburn we can point out a farmhouse, at no great distance, with whose thrifty matron no-one will yet dare to quarrel'.

Right: Barley. Witchcraft was still taking place round here last century.

Living in terror

But tales of witchcraft are not always quaint and comfortably distant in time. A former Burnley man is living in a seaside resort because he is in terror of a group of so-called witches that he once joined. An interest in magic had led him to consort with them in the first place, but he was disgusted at their rites and decided that this form of witchcraft at least was very definitely not for him.

Advertisements for witchcraft equipment are openly displayed nowadays in some magazines, but not all of them seem to be designed to attract people interested in what many believe to be an ancient religion. On such advert' asks for volunteers to join a coven and adds that full sexual instruction will be given. This is the sort of witchcraft so beloved by the seamier Sunday newspapers, with people justifying all sorts of squalid practices on the grounds that they are taking part in some historic ritual.

Another link with the days of Demdike that is still with us is possession by demons. Exorcisms are still carried out and churchmen still wrestle with evil spirits. As long as members of the clergy continue to claim to be able to cast out these demons, it seems certain that less reputable folk will go on claiming that they can put them there in the first place.

Secret rites

Those claiming to be witches still live and their ceremonies are one of the closest guarded secrets of today. Everyone has heard garbled stories of what goes on in witch covens, but very few know what really happens. There is no one "right" sort of witchcraft any more than there is any "right" form of Christianity. Witch ceremonies take different forms and there is no central organisation linking the various covens.

Many witches, and this term covers both men and women, believe that they are carrying on an ancient religion handed down from the days before Christianity. Although there have been moves among some witches to bring their practices into the open, the vast majority still shun publicity.

Persecuted

A Lancashire born witch speaks with a shudder of one of her colleagues in London who was featured in a Sunday newspaper. She says: "She has had a rough time since, despite living in cosmopolitan London. Her car had damage done to it, her telephone had to be monitored due to obscene calls, she was sent hundreds of letters and religious tracts, bricks were thrown through her house windows and children yell after her in the street. What a life. It almost broke her marriage. Her husband is a big noise in the City and was hoping to be elected president of his club, but was blackballed out. Do you wonder I lie low?"

The four Sabbats

The speaker, who was at one time high priestess of a coven which included her husband, also sheds light on the religious framework of witchcraft. She says that there are four main Sabbats: festivals which mark the natural seasons of the year. These are: Candlemas, the evening of January 31st; Walpurgis, the night of April 30th; Lammas, on the evening of July 31st; and—most sacred of all—Hallowe'en on October 31st.

On Hallowe'en, when thousands of folk from the towns round Pendle are making their annual pilgrimage to the hill, when, as the latterday witches say, the sun is dying and the earth is going to sleep, these witches offer up a ritualistic prayer asking that the sun be returned in the Springtime:

"Dread Lord of the shadows, god of life and the giver of life, yet is the knowledge of thee the knowledge of death. Open wide I pray thee thy gates, through which every man must pass. Let our dear ones who have gone before return this night to make merry with us, and when our time comes, as it must, oh thou the comforter, the giver of peace and rest, we will enter thy domains gladly and unafraid. For we know that when rested and refreshed among our dear ones we are born again into this life, with sturdier limbs and keener brains.

"By thy grace and by the grace of the great mother, let it be in the same place and at the same time as our beloved ones, and may we meet and know and remember and love them again. Descend we pray thee on thy servant and thy priest".

This Hallowe'en prayer touches on one of the central beliefs of witchcraft—reincarnation, for witches believe that after death they are reborn among people of their own kind.

The sabbats of witches are reserved for rituals, initiations and festivities; as a rule no magic is worked at them. Magic *is* worked, however, at the monthly meetings called Estbats. It seems that most witches nowadays meet indoors, probably to preserve their secrecy. Ceremonies are held near to the time of the full moon and involve members dancing naked.

But one thing most witches deny is that their religion has anything to do with perverting Christianity. Devil worship, the Black Mass and the Lord's Prayer said backwards have nothing to do with their ceremonies.

Familiars

All witches were supposed to have familiars — their own special demons in human or animal form—and Pendle's witches were no exception. The accounts of how each first met their familiars, and the relationships they enjoyed with them, make what is probably the most unbelievable part of the witches' story.

Old Demdike confessed that she had met her familiar in an old stone pit near Newchurch. The spirit, named Tib, was in the shape of a boy, dressed half in brown and half in black. Her daughter Elizabeth's familiar took the shape of a dog and was called Ball. James Device's was a black dog named Dandy, while Alizon's familiar was yet another black dog. Chattox's took the shape of a man called Fancy.

These familiars were supposed to appear at the witches' bidding to help them in their evil tasks, or to urge the women on to further wickedness, if such encouragement was needed.

Figments of the imagination

It has been surmised that these familiars might have been the secret partners witches take at their sabbats, but there is little evidence for this. More likely the familiars were the figments of their imaginations, or the imaginations of those who tried them. King James had laid down in his frequent statements on witchcraft that all witches had familiars, so the onus was certainly on people like Nowell to provide them.

So much then for Tib, Ball and Dandy. And for the most aptly named of all—Chattox's Fancy!

Lucky charms

"Chase the evil away by dint of sickle, horse shoe and hollow flint" goes an old rhyme describing the superstitious habits of Pendleside folk. For as long as men have believed in witches they have also believed in charms to ward off their evil powers.

Right: Horse shoes hang still at Bull Hole Farm where Demdike worked her magic.

and three of the most popular methods of protecting homes and stables were horse shoes, sickles, or hollow Hag stones hung near the door.

For a small sum people could obtain extra protection by getting someone with a little education to draw them up a charm, often in Latin, to be hung over their doors or their beds. One found near Burnley reads:

"Sun, Moon, Mars, Mercury, Jupiter, Venus, Saturn, Trine, Sextile, Dragon's Head, Dragon's Tail, I charge you to guard this house from all evil spirits whatever and guard it from all disorders and from anything being taken and give this family good health and wealth."

Other charms could be obtained to cure diseases, stop bleeding and other minor ills. A charm for curing warts was tried with success by one lady living today, after medical treatment—including burning the warts off—had failed. The charm was to cross each wart seven times on the first day, six times on the second day, five times on the third day, and so on until the course of treatment was complete, by which time the warts had vanished.

Warts and bed-wetting

A more messy remedy for warts involved stealing a piece of meat from a butchers' stall and after rubbing the parts affected with the stolen meat burying it under a gateway at a cross roads. Another remedy is to impale a snail on a thorn. As the snail wastes away so do the warts. An even simpler cure is to throw as many stones over your left shoulder as you have warts. The warts soon go, but whoever picks up the stones will develop them instead.

Some cures were particularly unpleasant, especially the practice of feeding young children on fried mice to stop them wetting their beds. Youngsters were better advised to have whooping cough, for the cure for this ailment was merely to wear a piece of string with nine knots in it tied round the neck.

Natural remedies

Many plants were supposed to possess virtues against illness or witchcraft, particularly the rowan tree, known as the "witchen tree". It was widely believed that no witch would come near to a rowan and that a small twig of it across a path barred the way to these workers of evil. Cattle could be protected by hanging rowan twigs over their stalls, and people could guarantee themselves a sound night's sleep by keeping a rowan branch handy. Pimpernel was another plant which was thought to be effective against witchcraft.

If a person felt himself directly under the influence of the evil eye stronger measures were needed. Drawing blood from a witch, especially from above the mouth, was the most popular method of combating this peril. Spitting three times in the witch's face, turning a live coal on the fire and simply calling out "The Lord be with us" were other remedies.

Chatterbox

We know what must be presumed to be a very effective charm from the lips of Chattox herself. The witch told magistrate Roger Nowell that a charm to prevent drinks being bewitched went thus:

"Three biters hast thou bitten,
The heart, ill eye, ill tongue,
Three bitter shall be thy boote,
Father, Sonne and Holy Ghost—a God's name,
Five Paternosters, five Avies and a Creede,
In a worship of five wounds of our Lord".

A complicated bit of nonsense, yet impressive. And therein lay the potency of spoken charms—not in the efficacy of the mumbo-jumbo *per se*, but in its power to awe and confuse.

Right: A charm against witchcraft found at Dawber's Farm, Foulridge.

A translation of the charm, provided by a cryptologist at The British Museum is as follows:

(Magical names or gibberish) . . . as it is said in the 17th chapter of Saint Matthew, beginning at the 20th verse; By faith ye shall remove mountains, may it be according to faith. If it be, or, shall be, that any . . . or demon resides in or disturbs this person or this place or this beast, I adjure thee in the name of the Father, the Son and the Holy Ghost (to depart) without any disturbance, trouble, or tumult whatsoever. So be it Our Father (then followed the Lord's Prayer).

The bounteous cow

Most of our Lancashire witches left little behind them, save a few lines of writing in some old document and a host of fanciful tales in the minds of the superstitious. But a more tangible reminder does remain, of a witch who once troubled the people of Longridge.

The mighty rib

Above the door of an old house at Halfpenny Lane, Longridge, above a carved inscription and the date 1616, hangs a strange, curved object, the rib bone of a giant cow. The beast, which was affectionately known as the Old Dun Cow, was the saviour of many villagers when drought struck the area one summer. The drought was so serious that it is said that even the wells dried up and people were going without food or water.

Milk into a sieve

The cow's owner, a benevolent farmer allowed his prodigious beast to wander the district so that these unfortunates could each take some milk from her—so large was the amount of milk that she produced. But one morning the villagers awoke to find the Witch of Longridge already milking the cow. Instead of using a beaker the old hag was using a sieve, which the kindly beast was doing its best to fill! After long hours the effort became too much for it and the animal fell down exhausted and died. Its passing was greatly mourned by the local people, who saved the rib as a memento.

The story of the Old Dun Cow has similarities with a much more famous tale about the Dun Cow of Warwick. This was another huge beast which could supply almost unlimited milk. But, enraged by man's greed, the cow turned wild and killed several people before being slain by Guy of Warwick. A memento of this beast also survives, in a tusk which is on display at Warwick Castle. Both legends live on in the popular inn name the "Dun Cow".

The "Witch" books

Harrison Ainsworth's novel "The Lancashire Witches" and Robert Neill's "Mist over Pendle" can be found on almost every

Right: The Dun Cow's rib at Longridge.

Lancashire bookshelf. Yet these books, which have done so much to popularise the tale of the Pendle Witches, could so easily have been joined by an account from one of Britain's greatest novelists, for it was Sir Walter Scott, author of books like "Ivanhoe" and the "Waverley Novels" who did much to revive interest in this piece of Lancashire's history.

Thomas Potts

The account of the witches' trial drawn up by Thomas Potts in 1613 had been forgotten by the beginning of the 19th century. It was Scott who rediscovered this historic document, republishing it in a book of "Scarce and Valuable Tracts". It seems amazing that a gifted and prolific writer like Scott should have let the basis for such an exciting story slip through his fingertips. But it was not until 35 years later, in 1845, that Potts' account came into the hands of a writer who saw its possibilities.

Harrison Ainsworth

In that year the Chetham Society, of Manchester, re-published the account, with an introduction by the society's president, James Crossley, a Manchester solicitor. Crossley's partner had a son—Harrison Ainsworth—who, though a qualified solicitor himself had forsaken the law for a career as a novelist. He had already scored his first success with the novel "Rookwood".

Crossley suggested that Ainsworth might write a romance from the account of the witchcraft trials, and it is obvious that the latter soon shared the solicitor's enthusiasm for the subject. Before long the young novelist was visiting North-East Lancashire, soaking up the Pendle atmosphere and collecting background information for the forthcoming book.

Ainsworth stayed at Newchurch-in-Pendle and Whalley, travelling round a countryside that could have changed little since the days of Demdike and Chattox. "The Lancashire Witches", published in 1848, was an outstanding success from the start and is still selling well.

Robert Neill

Early this century a boy named Robert Neill was growing up in Manchester. Born with a love of the countryside, he had a chance to escape from the smoke and industry of the city on visits to relatives in Colne. It was on these visits that he first

Right: Whalley Abbey which figures strongly
in Ainsworth's romantic version of the witches' tale.

saw Pendleside's beautiful scenery; scenery which the boy's inventive mind was not slow to populate with witches and other strange people; for with him he carried a copy of "The Lancashire Witches".

In spite of his reverence for Ainsworth's book, Neill felt there was still a Pendle Witches' story to be told. In 1951 his novel "Mist Over Pendle" appeared, giving a new twist to the famous tale. It has sold more than 160,000 copies in paperback and more than 30,000 hardback copies. A spokesman for the publishers told me: "It's the sort of book that could go on selling for ever" ... a tribute to Neill's writing and to the enduring appeal of the subject.

Neill himself says, "Every time I go past a shop cluttered with Pendle Witch souvenirs I feel guilty. At times it seems that the real story of the witches is likely to be forever buried beneath a tide of gimmicky dolls, plastic broomsticks and car stickers."

Edgar Peel and Pat Southern

Their book "The Trials of the Lancashire Witches" does much to restore the balance, being a closely researched, factual account of what actually took place, not only at the trials but elsewhere.*

Ephemera

It's a fact that wherever genuine interest is fostered commercialism is sure to follow. There can be no doubt that the Pendle Witch "industry" is already big business and likely to become very big business indeed. Novels, books and maps come and go, and a recent BBC television drama and documentary has ensured that interest in the witches has spread beyond the confines of North-East Lancashire. If there is doubt about the effectiveness of the spells cast by Demdike and Chattox in their own lifetimes, there can be none about the spell that their story exerts upon thousands of people around the world.

Natural amenity at risk

The Pendle area, worth a visit for its natural beauty alone. has now become a magnet for swarms of visitors who have read the "Lancashire Witches" or "Mist Over Pendle", want to walk in the footsteps of the witches and be held in thrall by the timeless atmosphere.

Far right: Robert Neil with the hill he has helped to make famous.

Right: Demdike and Chattox in the BBC film. The illustration on page 4 is from the same film.

42

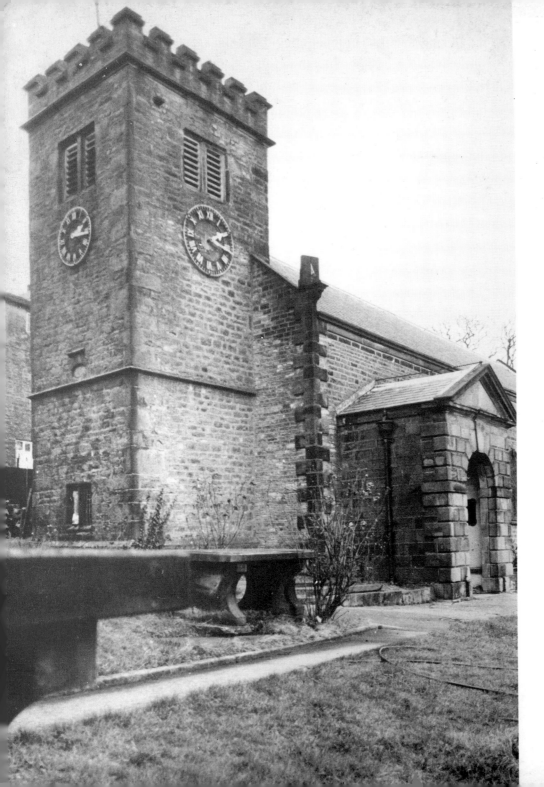

Local hoteliers report an increasing number of visitors, not only from Britain but from overseas: even the Japanese and Americans have discovered Pendle! Like it or not, and the countrylover will certainly have reservations about this, Pendle is becoming a tourist trap—a development which will affect the way of life of everyone in the area.

Can tiny roads cater for the inrush of visitors? Will their charm be spoiled by the building of bigger highways, or will there have to be restrictions on the number of vehicles using these roads? The Pendle country occupies only a precious few square miles of Lancashire. It is clear that if its beauty and character are to be preserved in the face of the mounting pressures on it, some form of management scheme must be initiated. If there is not, all that our children may be left of Pendle's special charm will be in the words and pictures of books such as this.

But although the Pendle area has seen many changes for the worse in the last few years, including ill-considered development on its fringes and even, in the case of Roughlee, in its very heart, most of its countryside is as unspoilt as ever.

Mystery and Imagination

Those who care to explore can find many of the places mentioned in the Pendle Witches' tale, old farms and old houses, like Greenhead and Bull Hole, and more magnificent dwellings, like Hoarstones, Gawthorpe Hall and Roughlee Hall. There is something to be seen at Newchurch where "The Eye of God" looks out of the church tower, where the Demdikes dug up buried corpses, and where the fanciful say dead witches lie.

In its subtle way, Pendle still retains its peculiar hold over people's imaginations and affections. On Good Friday thousands of walkers make the pilgrimage to its summit, but, more magical, is the great gathering on Hallowe'en when hordes of people trudge to the top. The darkness then is broken by myriad tiny lights and the mind turns naturally to tales of yesteryear, enabling this tale to end where it began — with the Pendle Witches.

Left: Newchurch Church with the "Eye of God" in the church tower.